Oh, Behave!

Manners Out and About

Siân Smith

www.raintreepublishers.co.uk
Visit our website to find out
more information about
Raintree books.

To order:
☎ Phone 0845 6044371
🖹 Fax +44 (0) 1865 312263
🖳 Email myorders@raintreepublishers.co.uk

Customers from outside the UK please telephone +44 1865 312262

Raintree is an imprint of Capstone Global Library Limited,
a company incorporated in England and Wales having its
registered office at 7 Pilgrim Street, London, EC4V 6LB
– Registered company number: 6695582

Edited by Dan Nunn, Rebecca Rissman, and John-Paul Wilkins
Designed by Marcus Bell
Picture research by Elizabeth Alexander
Production by Alison Parsons
Originated by Capstone Global Library Ltd
Printed and bound in China by Leo Paper Products Ltd

ISBN 978 1 406 23823 5
16 15 14 13 12
10 9 8 7 6 5 4 3 2 1

British Library Cataloguing in Publication Data
Smith, Siân.
Manners out and about. -- (Oh, behave!)
395.5'3-dc22
A full catalogue record for this book is available from the
British Library.

Acknowledgements
We would like to thank the following for permission to reproduce
photographs: © Capstone Publishers pp. 9, 10, 19, 22, 23 (Karon
Dubke); Alamy pp. 16, 23 (© Cultura Creative), 18, 22 (© SFL
Travel); Corbis pp. 5 (© moodboard), 7 (© Steve Hix/Somos
Images), 8 (© Yosuke Tanaka/Aflo), 14 (© Jim Craigmyle); Getty
Images pp. 11 (i love images/Cultura), 15 (Fuse); iStockphoto pp.
13 (© nautilus_shell_studios), 17 (© charlybutcher), 20 (© Rich
Legg), 21 (© Steve Debenport); Shutterstock pp. 4 (© Monkey
Business Images), 6 (© greenland), 12, 22 (© Ilya Andriyanov).

Front cover photograph of girl emptying cereal packet in a
supermarket reproduced with permission of Photolibrary (i love
images). Rear cover photograph of boy throwing away rubbish
reproduced with permission of iStockphoto (© charlybutcher).

Every effort has been made to contact copyright holders
of material reproduced in this book. Any omissions will be
rectified in subsequent printings if notice is given to the
publisher.

We would like to thank Nancy Harris and Dee Reid for their
assistance in the preparation of this book.

Contents

Good manners

People with good manners know
how to behave in different places.

If you have good manners, people will enjoy taking you out.

Show people your manners

Don't be rude when you speak
to people.

Say "please" and "thank you" when you ask for something.

Don't sit down if someone needs a seat more than you.

Ask if they would like your seat.

Don't push in front of people.

Wait your turn.

Don't pick your nose.

It is important not to touch things in some places.

Everywhere you go

litter

Never drop litter. Litter spoils places for everyone.

Put litter in a bin.

Don't put your feet on seats.

It will make them dirty for everyone.

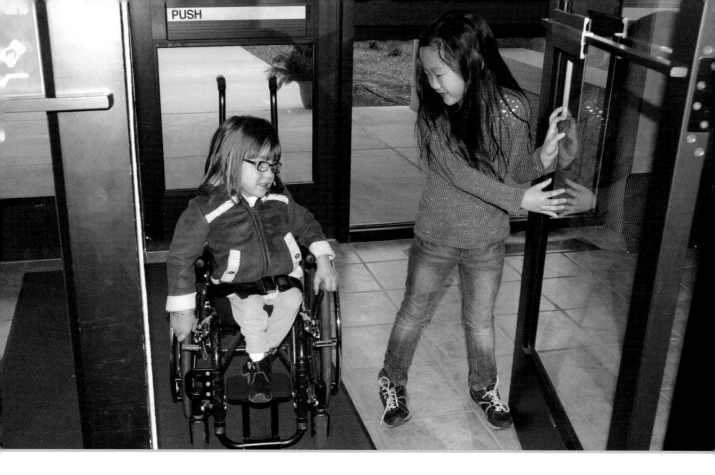

Hold doors open for other people.

Treat people the way you want to be treated.

People with good manners make the world a nicer place to be.

Best behaviour

Which person here has good manners?

Answer on page 24

Picture glossary

good manners ways of behaving politely and well

litter rubbish

Index

Answer to question on page 22
The girl holding the door open for someone has good manners.

Notes for parents and teachers

Before reading

Explain that good manners are ways of behaving – they help us to understand what to do and how to act. They are important because they show us how to treat each other and help us to get on well with other people. What examples of good manners can the children think of? List these together.

After reading

- Ask the children to share examples of good manners and bad manners they've seen when they have been out to different places. For any examples of bad manners, discuss together what that person should have done.
- Tell the children to imagine they are organizing a school trip (this could be for younger pupils). Divide the children into groups and ask each group to decide where they will go. Ask them to think about how the children they take will need to behave. Each group can decide what good manners tips they would give to the children on the trip.
- Give pairs or groups of children examples of good manners when out and about to role-play. Different groups can try this at the same time or groups could take turns and be given more support. Children can guess what is being shown and think about how the people in the role play would feel.